MW00959492

Summary:
The 4-Hour Body

Summary of the book by
Timothy Ferriss

by
Parker Publishing

Artificial Intelligence Notice

The author generated this text in part with OpenAI's large-scale language-generation models. Upon generating draft language, the author reviewed, edited, and revised the language to their own liking and takes ultimate responsibility for the content of this publication.

Table of Contents

Executive Summary

"The 4-Hour Body" by Timothy Ferriss introduces the concept of "Minimum Effective Dose" (MED), which means using the least amount of effort to achieve the intended results, especially in physical workouts.

Hormonal changes, metabolism, and proper use of drugs and supplements play crucial roles in achieving goals such as weight loss, fat loss, and muscle gain, termed "recomposition". Actions like a "Harajuku Moment", turning desires into needed changes for better health, can propel major life improvements.

Various tools and techniques are introduced for effective body monitoring, emphasizing the significance of consistent and accurate body fat measurements in weight management.

Principles like making habits conscious, creating competition, and setting small, attainable goals are highlighted as strategies for behavioral change towards more effective dieting, exercising, and overall health improvement.

The Slow-Carb Diet and the use of PAGG, a blend of natural supplements, are suggested as effective methods for fast weight loss. Other strategies discussed include cold exposure to increase calorie burn and blood glucose monitoring for insight into healthy eating habits.

Emphasis is given to injury prevention techniques, unconventional treatments for healing injuries, training methods to enhance athletic performance, and learning the right ways to exercise for better results.

Lastly, Ferriss suggests that significant lifestyle changes, leading to improved physical health, can improve mental and emotional health, productivity, and overall personal growth.

Chapter Summaries

The Minimum Effective Dose: From Microwaves to Fat-Loss

Main Idea

Arthur Jones established the "minimum effective dose" in exercise science, meaning the least effort that will produce a desired outcome. Overdoing it can be wasteful and harmful.

Summary

Arthur Jones, a pioneer in exercise science, developed the "minimum effective dose" (MED), a concept focusing on using the least effort needed to achieve a specific outcome.

Just as boiling water or getting a tan doesn't improve with more heat or sun, muscle training benefits most from MED. Using only enough effort to reach desired results saves time and prevents waste.

Achieving goals like physical change doesn't require doing more but rather using effort wisely. Overdoing it can be harmful. The challenge lies in resisting the temptation to do too much.

Understanding complex biology isn't necessary for applying MED. For example, a basic 80-second weight exercise can stimulate muscle growth without knowing all the biology behind it.

Precise measurement and control are crucial to applying MED effectively. For best results in exercise routines, rely on prescriptions based on MED.

Rules That Change the Rules: Everything Popular Is Wrong

Main Idea

Transforming health and fitness goes beyond mere calorie counting; it involves understanding metabolism, hormonal changes, recomposition, and the impact of diet composition on weight outcomes.

Summary

Losing weight is not just about cutting calories. Hormonal changes and metabolism are also important. Exercise doesn't burn many calories; heat therapy and hormonal changes can be more effective.

Drugs and supplements must be used safely. Even if something is "all-natural," it may not be safe.

The goal isn't just to lose weight but to change your appearance by adding muscle and losing fat. This is called "recomposition". The goal for most people over 120 pounds is 20 pounds of "recomposition".

"Recomposition" is usually achieved by 60% diet, 10% drugs, and 30% exercise. But this can change based on each person's needs.

It's important to know the difference between exercise and physical recreation. Exercise is planned and structured to meet health goals, while recreation is for fun and may not always improve health.

The Harajuku Moment: The Decision to Become a Complete Human

Main Idea

A "Harajuku Moment" is a crucial awakening that shifts a desire to a need, sparking profound changes in areas like health and wellness.

Summary

A "Harajuku Moment" is a turning point that changes a person's desires into needs, propelling major life improvements, like better health and fitness.

Chad Fowler, a tech executive, had a Harajuku Moment which changed his approach to health and fitness, starting with simple steps like improving his diet and cardio.

Fowler used data, like his Basal Metabolic Rate and calorie count, to set realistic weight loss goals. He didn't worry about the numbers being exact, just that they pointed him in the right direction.

Exercise became part of Fowler's everyday life. He combined it with chores and checked his heart rate often. He also hired a trainer to teach him the right exercises and help build muscle, which helps burn fat.

Fowler used biology and data in his weight loss journey. His methods included using clothes sizes as motivation, following stoic principles, and understanding how friends can influence our health goals.

Elusive Bodyfat: Where Are You Really?

Main Idea

Precise measurement tools, like DEXA, BodPod, and ultrasound, play a crucial role in tracking body transformation progress, ensuring a comprehensive understanding of body composition beyond just weight.

Summary

To transform your body, it's important to use precise tracking and measurement tools, not just scales.

Some useful tools for understanding your body composition are DEXA, BodPod, and BodyMetrix Ultrasound. Make sure to use the same tool consistently to accurately track progress.

When using bio-electrical impedance, maintain consistent hydration. If you're using calipers, use the same algorithm every time for accurate readings.

By measuring body fat accurately and regularly, people are more likely to manage their weight successfully. Don't forget to measure the circumference of your upper arms, waist, hips, and legs.

Lastly, there are specific body fat percentage goals for different body types. Despite how one looks physically, it's the body fat percentage that truly indicates their health status.

From Photos to Fear: Making Failure Impossible

Main Idea

Achieving daunting goals, such as fitness challenges, can be managed through behavior modification. This involves awareness, playing games or setting competitions, and making manageable changes and commitments.

Summary

Trevor lost over 40 pounds by creating a workout routine with a coworker and setting up penalties for skipping sessions, showing the power of routine and accountability.

Four behavior-changing principles are key: making habits conscious, making it like a game, creating competition, and starting with small, temporary goals.

A "flash diet" is suggested, which requires taking a photo of every meal before eating, using real-time feedback to boost awareness of food intake.

Encouragement was provided for using tools, like fat replicas for visual motivation, and online platforms, including Posterous and DailyBurn for sharing progress to help reach fitness goals.

The importance of making small changes, committing to them, and letting further decisions align with these ("consonant decisions") are emphasized as strategies to start and maintain a journey towards fitness.

The Slow-Carb Diet I: How to Lose 20 Pounds in 30 Days Without Exercise

Main Idea

The Slow-Carb Diet lets people lose significant body fat quickly. It consists of simple meals that repeat, avoids white carbs and fruit, and includes a weekly cheat day.

Summary

The Slow-Carb Diet helps people lose weight fast by changing their diet, exercise, and supplements. It has five main rules: avoiding white carbs and fruit, repeating the same few meals, not drinking many calories, and having one cheat day per week.

Each meal is about four hours apart and consists of proteins, legumes, and vegetables. Some examples are scrambled eggs with beans and vegetables for breakfast and organic beef, pinto beans, and mixed vegetables for lunch and dinner.

Common items on the grocery list for this diet are eggs, grass-fed organic beef, mixed vegetables, pork, chicken, pinto and black beans, peas, asparagus, and spinach.

Andrew, an active man who follows this diet, saves money by buying discounted items, shopping at smaller stores, and getting dried beans from a Mexican grocery store.

This diet is more about weight loss results than enjoyment. Stories like Andrew's prove that following the Slow-Carb Diet on a budget is possible.

.

The Slow-Carb Diet II: The Finer Points and Common Questions

Main Idea

The Slow-Carb Diet encourages high protein, beans and veggies intake, strategic cheat days, flavorful cooking with healthy oils, and minimal effective exercise for effective fat loss.

Summary

The Slow-Carb Diet involves rotating five or six distinct meals and designating one day per week as a "cheat day." Add potassium, magnesium, and calcium to your diet or take them as pills to replace the excess water loss from the diet. You'll gain weight after a cheat day but this is just water weight which typically disappears in two days.

Even if some people dislike beans, they are recommended in the diet. You can make them less bland by choosing lentils or organic beans, adding different condiments, or mixing them with other foods. Cooking with spices, herbs, and light sauces, using olive oil for low heat and grapeseed or macadamia oil for high-temperature cooking can make dishes more flavorful.

Beverages like dry wines are recommended, with red wine showing better fat-loss results. Limit snacks, and if really needed, opt for carrots or leftover restaurant food. A high-protein breakfast, like eggs, lentils, and spinach, can boost your metabolism by 20%.

To improve fat loss, have a spike in caloric intake once a week. This can also limit unplanned binges and have psychological benefits. Limiting the variety of veggies can simplify shopping and meal preparation, increasing the likelihood of following the diet.

When dieting, common mistakes include eating too late and not drinking enough water. Adding some targeted exercise can double fat loss and consumption of a high-protein breakfast within an hour of waking prevents evening overeating. Avoid foods that require portion control and don't consume artificial or natural sweeteners that encourage weight gain. Lastly, don't overdo gym workouts. The philosophy is less is more, only do the 'Minimum Effective Dose' (MED) of exercise for progress.

Damage Control: Preventing Fat Gain When You Binge

Main Idea

The author's experiment suggests that controlling insulin release, speeding up food digestion, and executing brief exercises before meals can manage weight despite high-calorie consumption.

Summary

The author challenges the idea that eating more calories simply leads to weight gain. He eats a lot of calories in a short time, and pays attention to how his body reacts.

To lessen the effects of overeating, the author uses three methods. One, he tries to limit the release of insulin. Two, he tries to make food leave his stomach faster. Three, he does brief exercises throughout his binge.

Here's how he does this: he starts the day eating a meal high in protein and fiber to control his hunger and follows with grapefruit juice to help control blood sugar. Also, he uses supplements to control insulin and drinks citrus juices.

To make food leave his stomach faster, he uses caffeine and Yerba Mate tea. This could help lessen the food that is stored as body fat.

The author does quick exercises like air squats and wall presses to help his muscles use more glucose. This is based on animal research about GLUT-4 proteins, which might help with weight loss.

The Four Horsemen of Fat-Loss: PAGG

Main Idea

PAGG, made from Policosanol, Alpha-lipoic acid, Green tea flavanols, and Garlic extract, is designed for weight loss. It works by targeting fat and preventing carb storage.

Summary

PAGG is a compound made from Policosanol, Alpha-lipoic acid (ALA), Green tea flavanols, and Garlic extract for fat loss. It was created as a safer alternative to the ECA method of weight loss which had harmful side effects.

Policosanol, part of PAGG, comes from plant waxes and can reduce body fat and improve cholesterol. Alpha-lipoic acid, another part, increases calorie absorption into muscles and treats type 2 diabetes.

Green tea flavanols in PAGG stop extra carbs from turning into fat and encourage fat cell death. Garlic Extract has allicin which stops fat from returning.

Allicin in Garlic Extract should disappear after six days, but it doesn't. This could be because of other parts, like S-Allyl cysteine. This is why aged garlic extract (AGE), which has all the parts, is used.

If you take PAGG, make sure to also take B-complex vitamins and talk to your doctor if you have medical conditions or take certain other medicines. It's unsafe for pregnant or breastfeeding women. The recommended PAGG supplements have no connection to the researcher.

Ice Age: Mastering Temperature to Manipulate Weight

Main Idea

Exposure to cold temperatures can enhance weight loss by activating brown adipose tissue (BAT), which burns calories. This could revolutionize fat-loss strategies.

Summary

Ray Cronise, a former NASA scientist, researched weight loss by studying how the body uses heat.

He used Olympic swimmer Michael Phelps as an example. Phelps eats a lot but doesn't gain weight, possibly because he spends so much time in cold water, which may increase calorie burn.

Cronise did an experiment where he exposed his body to cold temperatures, like drinking iced water. This helped him lose weight faster than just diet and exercise.

Through this, he found two important body tissues: white adipose tissue (WAT) and brown adipose tissue (BAT). BAT burns calories when it is cold, helping with weight loss.

Based on this, Cronise believes cold can increase BAT in the body. This could potentially change how people approach weight loss in the future.

The Glucose Switch: Beautiful Number 100

Main Idea

Testing specific food and activities with a Continuous Glucose Monitor (CGM) helps understand their effects on blood glucose levels and overall health, optimizing diets and exercise routines.

Summary

The author uses a device, DexCom SEVEN, to see how different foods and activities affect blood glucose levels. This helps him understand the healthiest diet and exercise plan.

His results show that the glycemic index is flexible. What raises blood sugar in one person may not in another. The data suggests a high-fat diet can balance blood glucose levels.

Food takes longer to reach the bloodstream than he thought. This affects when and what to eat before and after workouts. Meals high in healthy fat caused less increase in glucose levels.

Fructose lowers blood glucose but doesn't necessarily lead to fat loss. Vinegar did not lower glucose levels, while lemon juice and cinnamon did. The size and speed of eating a meal also affect glucose levels.

The author introduces several tools for health monitoring, like the WaveSense Jazz glucometer and the Glucose Buddy app. He recommends making changes to meals, such as adding in cinnamon and lemon juice, and eating meat that hasn't been treated.

The Last Mile: Losing the Final 5–10 Pounds

Main Idea

Achieving sub-10% body fat can be challenging. High-Intensity Training, a protein-focused 'Jumbo' Palumbo diet, and cautious use of performance-enhancing drugs can help, despite possible risks.

Summary

Losing the final few pounds to hit sub-10% body fat is difficult but can be achieved with natural and chemical methods.

John Romano, a fitness expert, believes in High-Intensity Training (HIT), a specific diet, and some drugs to help improve health and fitness levels.

The 'Jumbo' Palumbo diet, a method suggested by Romano, includes eating 8 ounces of protein every three hours along with some healthy fats, which assists in losing body fat.

If diet and training don't get you to your goal, Romano suggests some drugs may help achieve body fat levels of less than 4% but warns of the high health risks from misuse.

Preparing as an advanced bodybuilder takes patience and includes a special diet, dedicated training, practicing posing, and disciplined use of performance-enhancing drugs. This approach is effective but risky.

.

Building the Perfect Posterior (or Losing 100+ Pounds)

Main Idea

Weight loss and body transformation are achievable quickly through targeted exercises and diet changes, focusing on the muscles from your neck to your heels.

Summary

The story starts with Tracy Reifkind, a woman who lost over 100 pounds using a Russian kettlebell swing and other lifestyle changes that primarily targeted her posterior chain, a group of muscles stretching from her neck to her ankles.

A man named "The Kiwi" used weighted swings to reshape a woman's body in just four weeks, emphasizing the effectiveness of targeted exercises for body transformation.

By using the kettlebell swing, one can perform a minimalistic exercise routine that significantly reduces body fat, supporting the idea of "more results from less work".

It is important to track progress not just by scale weight, but also self-measurements, as shown by the example of Fleur, who made considerable changes in her body proportions and posture through exercise.

Tracy's successful weight loss journey, featuring a combination of regular exercise with kettlebells, nutrition adjustments, and a weekly cheat meal, highlights the principles of discipline, simplicity, and targeted efforts.

Six-Minute Abs: Two Exercises That Actually Work

Main Idea

Visible six-pack abs are developed through the Myotatic Crunch and the Cat Vomit Exercise, accompanying a diet that maintains low bodyfat.

Summary

The Myotatic Crunch is an exercise that helps shape six-pack abs. It uses a BOSU or Swiss ball for movement and focuses on stretching the back muscles.

The Cat Vomit Exercise works the "corset muscle", an abdominal muscle that runs horizontally. It involves deep breathing and repeating a cycle of movements 10 times.

Eating a diet that keeps body fat 12% or less is key to making abs visible. Diets like Slow-Carb, ketogenic, and intermittent fasting can work.

For women who want to keep their hourglass shape, timed planks are suggested. Planks strengthen hip muscles and help maintain the hourglass figure.

Daily hip flexor stretches are also recommended for women. These stretches help enhance lower body shape and support abdominal workouts.

From Geek to Freak: How to Gain 34 Pounds in 28 Days

Main Idea

Quality and intensity of workouts can override genetics for muscle development, achievable through strategic exercises, recovery time, and efficient gym time usage.

Summary

The author managed to gain 34 pounds of muscle in 28 days by focusing on the quality and intensity of his workouts instead of the duration.

Despite his genetics not being naturally inclined for muscle growth, he was able to change this through specific workouts and lifestyle alterations.

He crafted a workout plan with four key parts: doing one set of each exercise to the point of muscle failure, maintaining a careful slow pace, doing 2-10 different exercises every workout, and increasing rest time as muscles grow.

His methods were built off the Colorado Experiment, a muscle-building experiment with bodybuilder Casey Viator that emphasized targeted workouts.

He affirms that achieving weight goals doesn't require more than four hours at the gym each month, but rather making the most out of each minute spent exercising.

Occam's Protocol I: A Minimalist Approach to Mass

Main Idea

The Occam's Protocol, a simplified workout approach, aims for muscle growth and strength using minimal gym time, controlled routines, and a specific eating plan with supplements.

Summary

The author and Neil Strauss used the 'Occam's Protocol' aimed at gaining 10 pounds of muscle in four weeks. They faced challenges but also had successes such as eating more food without feeling sick.

The "Bike Shed Effect," is introduced, a concept about people giving unwelcome advice. The takeaway is to ignore distractions from others during your fitness journey.

The 'Occam's Protocol' is a simple workout routine done in under 30 minutes a week. It involves two sets of two primary lifts until muscle failure, focusing on lift speed and shoulder safety.

The author gives safe techniques for bench presses to avoid shoulder injuries. He provides two routines (workout A and B) with specific instructions and options for free weights or machines for travelers.

The author introduces 'Occam's Feeding', regular meals for effective muscle gain, and techniques to boost weight gain. Recommended supplements include Cissus Quadrangularis, Alpha-lipoic acid, L-glutamine, and creatine monohydrate.

Occam's Protocol II: The Finer Points

Main Idea

The Occam's Protocol II fitness regimen emphasizes the importance of consistent workouts with specific weights, necessary nutrient intake and rest. Its objective is muscle growth over strength.

Summary

"Occam's Protocol II" is a fitness regimen that determines starting weights based on five-repetition sets. If you can't do five reps, lower the weight. The starting point is 70% of the last successful set (60% for shoulder press).

If you reach the minimum reps, add 10 pounds or 10% total weight in your next workout. If you don't reach the minimum, you may need more rest or food. Wait 48 hours, then try again.

The protocol does not encourage calorie counting unless weight gain is an issue. Instead, it recommends eating 20 calories per pound of lean bodyweight for 10 pounds more than your current weight. This can be tracked over 24-hour periods.

The regimen enhances both anaerobic and aerobic fitness without making you slower. Other techniques include minimal warm-ups, consistent rest periods, avoiding trying too hard, and focusing on specific goals.

The regime primarily targets tissue growth for muscle gain. If gains slow, you can split the routine for better results. This routine also increases strength, helping gym-goers push pass their limits. It is important to understand your fitness goals and keep a precise training for best results.

Sex Machine I: Adventures in Tripling Testosterone

Main Idea

Increasing testosterone and libido depends on dietary changes, hormone manipulation, and nutrient supplementation, including managing vitamin D and cholesterol levels individually.

Summary

The author conducts experiments to increase testosterone levels, using diet changes, hormones, and nutrients. This boosts his sexual desire and aggression.

The author learns that increasing luteinizing hormone levels, not testosterone injections, raises libido. This leads to two strategies: a long-term plan for steady growth and a short-term 'boost'.

Part of these strategies includes eating cholesterol-rich foods at night for testosterone and lowering the hormone that prevents testosterone from working.

The author also uses different supplements like vitamin D and cod liver oil for good health and hormone control. He recommends getting tested for deficiency or imbalance before making big diet changes.

The author also experiments with a high-fat diet, discovering it improved his cholesterol levels and overall health. This overturns the idea that high cholesterol is bad, showing instead that balanced cholesterol is key.

Happy Endings and Doubling Sperm Count

Main Idea

Falling sperm counts in men might be due to environmental factors or cellphone radiation. One solution is sperm banking for future fertility insurance.

Summary

Dr. Louis Guillette shared research showing that sperm counts in men from industrialized countries are dropping about 1% each year since 1942. This happens even in healthy men from various factors like environmental pollutants, tight underwear, or unknown causes.

The writer of the book, with his own low sperm count, decided to see if radiation from cellphones affects sperm quality. He moved his cellphone away from his body. After 11 weeks, his sperm count nearly tripled.

While he cannot prove that moving his cellphone was the only reason for the sperm count increase, he suggests that avoiding potential risks merits consideration. He started cold treatments and selenium supplementation around the same time.

He shares other possible risks to male fertility, such as diet, toxins, medical conditions, and personal changes. He advises men to consider banking sperm as a way to avoid future fertility problems.

He ends with sharing his own decision to bank his sperm for possible future children and provides details on the process. He concludes with a list of resources for finding a reliable sperm bank and learning more about threats to male reproductive health.

Engineering the Perfect Night's Sleep

Main Idea

Factors like REM sleep, alcohol, pre-bed snacks, room temperature, pre-bedtime meal, and body position affect sleep quality and falling asleep time.

Summary

The author struggled with severe insomnia, a problem they shared with their family, and decided to study sleep patterns with motion detectors and gadgets.

From this study, they learned how REM sleep, alcohol, and pre-bed snacks impacted sleep quality and physical performance.

Room temperature and certain foods also affected how fast they fell asleep, suggesting readers try different meals and climates.

They experienced better sleep from high-protein meals before bed, blue-light in the morning, strength training, cold baths before sleep, and using specific products like the Air-O-Swiss Humidifier and NightWave pulse light.

Some other effective tools were the F.lux application, California Poppy Extract, Zeo Personal Sleep Coach device, and Sleep Cycle iPhone App. Lucid dreaming, with the help of huperzine-A, also improved sleep quality.

Becoming Uberman: Sleeping Less with Polyphasic Sleep

Main Idea

Polyphasic sleep divides sleep into various segments throughout the day to heighten alertness and productivity, maximize REM sleep, and potentially lessen total sleep time.

Summary

Polyphasic sleep is a way to split sleep into segments throughout the day. This could shrink sleep time down to just two hours, but keep you alert and productive.

Some people, like Thomas Edison, used polyphasic sleep to have more awake hours. Some commonly used methods are "Everyman" and "Siesta." In emergencies, some people use the "Uberman" method, which only includes six short naps.

The goal of polyphasic sleep is to get more REM sleep. REM is the most beneficial sleep phase. You try to trick your body into entering REM more often by sleeping for shorter periods.

The Uberman method is the most strict. You only sleep for two hours total, but you must take your naps at the planned times. If you miss a nap, you could feel tired for days.

If you want to follow a polyphasic sleep schedule, you must make a sleep schedule, avoid sleeping in, not skip naps, and get through the tough beginning phase. You might also use tools to keep track of when you sleep.

Reversing "Permanent" Injuries

Main Idea

The author successfully reversed his athletic injuries using non-traditional therapies like shoe heel removal, yoga, the Egoscue method, and Advanced Muscle-Integration Therapy, despite significant setbacks.

Summary

The author suffered from long-term injuries due to strenuous athletic activities and sought non-traditional treatments to heal himself. His trials were costly and dangerous, with some leading to further injuries.

After many setbacks, he found relief with unconventional therapies such as shoe heel removal, Vibram shoe training, Feldenkrais exercises, Pilates, assisted stretching, Tai Chi Chuan, and Yoga. He also learned the importance of foot alignment and the right footwear in preventing physical damage.

The Egoscue Method, developed by Peter Egoscue, was beneficial in fixing the author's posture. The method uses special exercises to relieve body pain and improve posture. Using it, the author found relief from persistent mid-back pain.

Another effective therapy was the Advanced Muscle Integration Therapy (AMIT). This method works on the principle that the body deactivates muscles when injured to avoid further damage. AMIT reactivates these dormant muscles, reducing strain and relieving pain.

Finally, the author found success with the Active Release Technique (ART), a manual muscle manipulation method, and Prolotherapy, a pain treatment involving injection of irritants into tissues. Despite the high costs and risks involved, these treatments improved his muscle strength, range of motion, and chronic pain. He also recognized that a nutrient-dense diet can help alleviate inflammation and abnormal calcium deposits in tissues.

How to Pay for a Beach Vacation with One Hospital Visit

Main Idea

Medical tourism can save money and time, providing quality care and preventive tests like MRIs without wait time. Resources can guide affordable global healthcare choices.

Summary

The story centers around a person who goes to Nicaragua to enjoy a beach vacation and get cheaper medical services.

He goes through multiple medical procedures, including 7 MRIs, blood tests, and urine testing, which turn out to be much cheaper than back in San Francisco.

The medical services in Nicaragua are just as good if not better than in the U.S., and there is no waiting period like in his home country. This proves to be more convenient and hassle-free.

The story implores others to view medical tourism as a means to not just timely surgeries or beautification, but also preventive care, showing the significance of MRIs in finding health issues early.

The story ends by sharing resources to help find the best global medical services at reasonable prices, mentioning a book, a medical tourism guide and some website references.

Pre-Hab: Injury-Proofing the Body

Main Idea

Preventing injury through 'pre-hab' is key. This involves identifying and correcting body imbalances using the Functional Movement Screen (FMS) system and associated exercises.

Summary

'Pre-hab' is a way to avoid injuries before they happen. You must balance your body's strength before building muscle or increasing speed.

Injury prevention expert Gray Cook uses the Functional Movement Screen (FMS). It finds imbalance in the body which helps prevent injuries.

Avoiding imbalance is key to staying injury-free. Anyone can get hurt if their movements lack stability. The FMS system uses exercises like deep squats and lunges to find and fix these imbalances.

To get the most from the FMS system, it should be done regularly. Focusing on balance and coordination is more important than becoming stronger.

While using this system, it's important to use correct techniques, like using bars for exercises. Correct breathing is also necessary. These activities should be recorded for tracking progress. The idea is to find weak areas and improve them for better balance. Any differences more than 10% between left and right sides are called imbalances.

Hacking the NFL Combine I: Preliminaries—Jumping Higher

Main Idea

Innovative training at Joe DeFranco's gym significantly boosts athletes' performance, particularly for the NFL Scouting Combine, affecting their potential pay.

Summary

The author joined Joe DeFranco's gym, where athletes train for the NFL Scouting Combine, a critical event where top NFL coaches assess college football players. DeFranco is famous for his unconventional methods that help athletes succeed in tests like the vertical jump and 40-yard dash.

Correcting any existing flaws, such as a bad shoulder drive or a too-wide squat stance, can help improve an athlete's performance. The author saw significant improvements in his vertical jump and 40-yard dash time after training at DeFranco's gym.

Good performance at the NFL Scouting Combine can greatly increase an athlete's pay. Many sports agents promise training with DeFranco to attract the best players.

DeFranco employs a range of tools and tricks like unique warm-up techniques, physical tests, and even horse liniment to train the athletes.

The chapter also highlights the extraordinary athletic performance of Keith Eloi, illustrating the potential of human endurance and athleticism. His training and discipline are provided as resources on a website for those interested.

Hacking the NFL Combine II: Running Faster

Main Idea

Improving sprint speed requires correct techniques, body position, and warm-ups. It also involves recognizing injury signs and adopting preventive measures to support healthier exercise habits.

Summary

Strength coach Joe DeFranco shares how to improve sprint speed with techniques focused on body position and foot placement. He used ideas from Charlie Francis, who coached gold medallist Ben Johnson, about short distance sprints at high effort.

DeFranco explains how to increase starting speed by adjusting hand, arm and foot placements. This allows runners to push off more forcefully at the start of their sprint.

To run more efficiently, your body should lean forward, your head should be down, and you should aim to take fewer steps. Using these tips, the author improved his 10-yard sprint time.

Sprinting comes with injury risks, like a pulled hamstring. It's important to recognize injury signs early, and not to try fixing it by stretching. Instead, use ice and Arnica Montana, a plant with anti-inflammatory properties.

Preventing injuries is key, especially hamstring pulls, which can occur when your torso stands too upright in sprints.

Regularly stretch hip flexors, and do exercises like glute-ham raises and hip thrusts to strengthen your body and protect against injuries.

Ultraendurance I: Going from 5K to 50K in 12 Weeks—Phase I

Main Idea

Optimizing body position, increasing neuromuscular efficiency, and incorporating high-intensity workouts, drastically improves running endurance, highlighting the significance of proper form and injury-avoiding biomechanics.

Summary

Kelly Starrett and Brian MacKenzie introduce a unique running endurance method. It is about having a good body position and reducing distance for better efficiency and speed, instead of traditional aerobic training.

Using high-intensity workouts like 400-meter repeats and weightlifting, the method enables the body to maintain a good pace. It helps improve running abilities quickly.

Proper running form is vital to prevent injuries and boost performance, emphasizing this method is not only effective but time-efficient.

Training for long races involves focusing on the body's ligaments and tendons. It's important that these are robust and that muscles work in the right way.

The Pose Method by Nicolas S. Romanov, which involves using gravity for forward motion and landing on the balls of the feet, is introduced. This technique improves running mechanics and suggests keeping a 180-step minute rate for effective muscle elasticity.

Ultraendurance II: Going from 5K to 50K in 12 Weeks—Phase II

Main Idea

Brian's 12-week training regimen can help runners increase endurance significantly by focusing on glycogen storage, energy sourced from fat, and mastering the lactic acid system.

Summary

Brian, an experienced coach, helps athletes, especially runners, to upgrade their endurance to run a 50K race. He does this by training the body to use fat as an energy source instead of glycogen.

Brian's training program doesn't exceed 13.1 miles in any run and aims to enhance all energetic pathways, particularly the lactic acid system. It also teaches muscles to stay aerobic at high speed levels, promoting endurance recovery.

During the 12-week training program, runners should follow a Paleo diet to stay fueled. But after workouts, a carbohydrate supplement is allowed. It's also important to keep a recovery heart rate of less than 120 beats in two minutes.

Brian's program warns against barefoot running and lifting toes while running which can hurt the Achilles tendon and tibialis anterior muscle. He stresses keeping a steady stride rate when tired to keep good form.

To maintain energy during long races, runners start with Vitargo before switching to whole foods. Training also includes learning to eat while running and drinking a gram of carbs per kilogram of body weight each hour, but not all at once. Drinking a lot of water helps with digestion.

Effortless Superhuman: Breaking World Records with Barry Ross

Main Idea

Strength is a skill that can be rapidly improved with correct techniques, yielding significant results in short time periods. This principle applies to both general strength training and specific areas such as sprinting.

Summary

Pavel Tsatsouline, a former Soviet Special Forces instructor, believes strength is a skill you can learn quickly with the right techniques.

One example of Pavel's methods is when he helped someone increase their one-arm overhead press by 26% in under five minutes.

Barry Ross is a sprint coach known for training Allison Felix, who broke high school records at 17 and turned professional in track right after high school.

Ross aims to make people run fast. His athletes, who lift for less than 15 minutes each week, can lift more than two times their weight and gain less than 10% additional body weight.

The key to Ross's training is research that shows more force on the ground, not shorter leg swing times, makes you run faster. He thinks more tension needs more strength, and a stronger runner, all else being the same, will always win.

Eating the Elephant: How to Add 100 Pounds to Your Bench Press

Main Idea

Improving bench press skills involves systematic training, like Gallagher's three-phased plan, proper form, having a spotter, and drawing lessons from successful powerlifters.

Summary

DeFranco, a trainer, shares his techniques and tales of top powerlifters like Ceklovsky and Mendelson to show how strength training can boost bench press capability.

Using Gallagher's formula, fitness enthusiasts can potentially add 100 pounds to their bench press in six months if they're already capable of benching 200 pounds.

Gallagher's three-phase, 26-week training plan focuses first on boosting muscle mass, then on stabilizing gains, and finally on increasing bench press capacity.

To achieve the best bench press, trainers suggest tensing legs and glutes, tight gripping the bar, and controlling the movement to and from the chest. This strategy should push fatigue after 20 seconds.

Safety is crucial during bench press sessions. Use a spotter for assistance, maintain correct body position, and press the bar in the shortest line possible upwards. Minor elbow flaring could help with full extension if needed.

How I Learned to Swim Effortlessly in 10 Days

Main Idea

The author, once afraid and unfit at swimming, became competent and relaxed using the Total Immersion method, and encourages others to do the same.

Summary

The author struggled with swimming, resulting in stress and embarrassment, even though he was skilled in other sports.

A friend's challenge to swim a one-kilometer race pushed him to learn, with aid like kickboards providing little help. Instead, he found success with Total Immersion (TI), a technique by Terry Laughlin to reduce water resistance and number of strokes, improving the swimming experience.

He shares eight beneficial principles for new swimmers, like how to move, float level, control breathing, and focus on stroke length instead of speed.

The author recommends gear like tight swimwear and good goggles. He advises starting in a short, shallow pool and gradually moving to greater depths and lengths. He goes from hating to loving swimming and successfully swims long distances.

Overcoming his fear, he swam a mile alone in the ocean and experienced great pride and a Zen-like calmness. He attributes his transformation to TI training and provides resources like a DVD, favourite goggles, a demonstration video, and a website to find worldwide public swimming facilities. He encourages everyone to believe they can also become confident swimmers.

The Architecture of Babe Ruth

Main Idea

Jaime Cevallos's baseball coaching method improves batting technique and performance via focusing on three key aspects: The Cushion, The Slot, and Impact Position.

Summary

Jaime Cevallos, a baseball coach, improved his students' batting techniques by focusing on three main details: "The Cushion" for optimal power, "The Slot" for better home-run chances, and "Impact Position" for a more effective swing.

Cevallos measures a player's swing using a method called CSR (Cevallos Swing Rating). A higher CSR represents a powerful and consistent swing.

Cevallos also uses the Area of Impact (AOI) to determine the consistency of a player's swinging technique. A longer AOI means a player will likely hit the ball more consistently.

The use of the MP30 Training Bat, which helps batters to use the Slot position, is rising in popularity in major leagues due to its effectiveness. The Sports Radar Gun is also used to measure various metrics in sports activities, such as pitch speed in baseball.

A book entitled "Moneyball: The Art of Winning an Unfair Game" discusses the success of the Oakland Athletics in 2002 despite a low payroll. The team's success is credited to their use of statistical analysis in selecting players, highlighting the importance of data in sports decision-making.

How to Hold Your Breath Longer Than Houdini

Main Idea

David Blaine developed a method for holding one's breath for extended periods which involves specific breathing exercises, seating positions, and mental distractions.

Summary

Magician David Blaine practiced magic and endurance art from a young age, performing acts like standing on an 83-foot-tall column.

Blaine decided to hold his breath for a world record. After training hard, he succeeded with a time of 17 minutes and 4.4 seconds.

Seeing Blaine's success, the author learned to improve his own breath-holding skills. He trained with Blaine and beat Harry Houdini's record of 3.5 minutes.

The "David Blaine Method" for breath-holding is explained. This involves safe practice, certain exercises and techniques to reduce fear.

For those wanting to learn more about breath-holding and freediving, tools and resources are suggested. These include David's TEDMED talk, a freediving school, a book, and a handheld training device.

Living Forever: Vaccines, Bleeding, and Other Fun

Main Idea

Increasing lifespan and improving quality of life can be achieved through diet control, risk avoidance, low-risk therapies, and managing iron levels in the body.

Summary

Research showed that restricting calories in monkeys can extend their lifespan. One monkey on a diet lived longer than another monkey that ate freely.

Some strategies for living longer might be hard to follow in daily life because they require giving up things that make life enjoyable. For example, one study found that nematodes, a type of worm, lived shorter lives if they released too much sperm.

To live longer, it's important to avoid taking unnecessary risks. Instead, find joy in everyday things and do things that are known to improve life quality.

Risky therapies can cause unwanted side effects. Safer choices for living longer can include taking creatine monohydrate, a supplement, and fasting for certain periods.

The goal should be to extend life while also improving life quality. It's important not to give up basic needs and pleasures just to live longer. For example, it can help to donate blood regularly to reduce iron levels, which can potentially lower the risk of heart attacks and cancer. This can also help remove harmful pollutants from the body.

Even if certain pleasures, such as eating a favorite meal, might shorten life slightly, they can make life more enjoyable. Resources are available to learn more about how to live longer and how to reduce high iron levels.

Closing Thoughts: The Trojan Horse

Main Idea

Self-reinvention through physical transformation, like in endurance activities or strength gain, influences mental and emotional states, boosting confidence, productivity and overall wellbeing.

Summary

Physical trials such as ultramarathons can lead to personal growth, even if they are physically tough.

Changes in physical health, like weight loss or strength gain, can also improve general wellbeing. One example is the author's father becoming healthier after losing weight.

The book warns against thinking you're only "partially complete" due to self-imposed limits or excuses.

A strong, fit body can boost mental confidence and productivity. Good physical health can lead to improvements in mental and emotional health.

The book says you can change your life by changing your physical health, like those who defied age and physical limits. Use physical goals as a guide for life changes.

Made in the USA
Las Vegas, NV
06 November 2023

80348381R00049